Pursue the Cause of Liberty

Ludwig von Mises Institute
518 West Magnolia Avenue
Auburn, Ala. 36832
mises.org

ISBN: 978-1-61016-556-3

PURSUE THE CAUSE OF LIBERTY

A Farewell to Congress

Ron Paul

MISES
INSTITUTE

AUBURN, ALABAMA

Contents

Let me tell you: the work of the Mises Institute is crucial. This is important. This is more important than all political action. We have to change people's hearts and minds, and their understanding of free markets and individual liberty. That's how we change the world.

—Ron Paul, at the
30th Anniversary of the
Ludwig von Mises Institute

Introduction

ONE OF THE MOST THRILLING MEMORIES OF
the 2012 campaign was the sight of those
huge crowds who came out to see Ron. His
competitors, meanwhile, couldn't fill half a
Starbucks. When I worked as Ron's chief
of staff in the late 1970s and early 1980s, I
could only dream of such a day.

Now what was it that attracted all these
people to Ron Paul? He didn't offer his fol-
lowers a spot on the federal gravy train.
He didn't pass some phony bill. In fact, he
didn't do any of the things we associate with
politicians. What his supporters love about
him has nothing to do with politics at all.

Ron is the anti-politician. He tells unfashionable truths, educates rather than flatters the public, and stands up for principle even when the whole world is arrayed against him.

Some people say, "I love Ron Paul, except for his foreign policy." But that foreign policy reflects the best and most heroic part of who Ron Paul is. Peace is the linchpin of the Paulian program, not an extraneous or dispensable adjunct to it. He would never and could never abandon it.

Here was the issue Ron could have avoided had he cared only for personal advancement.

But he refused. No matter how many times he's been urged to keep his mouth shut about war and empire, these have remained the centerpieces of his speeches and interviews.

Of course, Ron Paul deserves the Nobel Peace Prize. In a just world, he would also win the Medal of Freedom, and all the honors for which a man in his position is eligible.

But history is littered with forgotten politicians who earned piles of awards handed out by other politicians. What matters to Ron more than all the honors and ceremonies in the world is all of you, and your commitment to the immortal ideas he has championed all his life.

It's Ron's truth-telling and his urge to educate the public that should inspire us as we carry on into the future.

It isn't a coincidence that governments everywhere want to educate children. Government education, in turn, is supposed to be evidence of the state's goodness and its concern for our well-being. The real explanation is less flattering. If the government's propaganda can take root as children grow up, those kids will be no threat to the state apparatus. They'll fasten the chains to their own ankles.

H.L. Mencken once said that the state doesn't just want to make you obey. It tries to make you want to obey. And that's one thing the government schools do very well.

A long-forgotten political thinker, Étienne de la Boétie, wondered why people would ever tolerate an oppressive regime. After all, the people who are governed vastly outnumber the small minority doing the governing. So the people governed could put a stop to it all if only they had the will to do so. And yet they rarely do.

De la Boétie concluded that the only way any regime could survive was if the public consented to it. That consent could range all the way from enthusiastic support to stoic resignation. But if that consent were ever to vanish, a regime's days would be numbered.

And that's why education—real education—is such a threat to any regime. If the state loses its grip over your mind, it loses the key to its very survival.

The state is beginning to lose that grip. Traditional media, which have carried water for the government since time began, it seems, are threatened by independent voices on the Internet. I don't think anyone under 25 even reads a newspaper.

The media and the political class joined forces to try to make sure you never found out about Ron Paul. When that proved impossible, they smeared him, and told you no one could want to go hear Ron when they could hear Tim Pawlenty or Mitt Romney instead.

All this backfired. The more they panicked about Ron, the more drawn to him people were. They wanted to know what it was that the Establishment was so eager to keep them from hearing.

Ours is the most radical challenge to the state ever posed. We aren't trying to make the state more efficient, or show how it can take in more revenue, or change its pattern of wealth redistribution. We're not saying that this subsidy is better than that one, or that this kind of tax would make the system run more smoothly than that one. We reject the existing system root and branch.

And we don't oppose the state's wars because they'll be counterproductive or overextend the state's forces. We oppose them because mass murder based on lies can never be morally acceptable.

So we don't beg for scraps from the imperial table, and we don't seek a seat at that table. We want to knock the table over.

We have much work to do. Countless Americans have been persuaded that it's in their interest to be looted and ordered around by a ruling elite that in fact cares nothing for their welfare and seeks only to increase its power and wealth at their expense.

The most lethal and anti-social institution in history has gotten away with describing itself as the very source of civilization. From the moment they set foot in the government's schools, Americans learn that the state is there to rescue them from poverty, unsafe medicines, and rainy days, to provide economic stimulus when the economy is poor, and to keep them secure against shadowy figures everywhere. This view is reinforced, in turn, by the broadcast and print media.

If the public has been bamboozled, as Murray Rothbard would say, it is up to us to do the de-bamboozling. We need to tear the benign mask off the state.

If it is through propaganda that people thoughtlessly accept the claims of the state, then it is through education that people must be brought to their senses.

With its kept media on the wane, it is going to be more and more difficult for the state to make its claims stick, to persuade people to keep accepting its lies and propaganda.

You've heard it said that the pen is mightier than the sword. Think of the sword as the state. Think of the pen as all of you, each in your own way, spreading the ideas of liberty.

Remember that insight of Étienne de la Boétie: all government rests on public consent, and as soon as the public withdraws that consent, any regime is doomed.

This is why they fear Ron, it's why they fear you, and it's why, despite the horrors

we read about every day, we may dare to
look to the future with hope.

—Llewellyn H. Rockwell, Jr.
Auburn, Alabama

Pursue the Cause of Liberty

THIS MAY WELL BE THE LAST TIME I SPEAK ON the House Floor. At the end of 2012, I'll leave Congress after 23 years in office over a 36-year period. My goals in 1976 were the same as they are today: promote peace and prosperity by a strict adherence to the principles of individual liberty.

It was my opinion, that the course the U.S. embarked on in the latter part of the twentieth century would bring us a major financial crisis and engulf us in a foreign

---

RON PAUL's "Farewell to Congress" a clarion call for education in Austrian economics and liberty, was delivered in the House of Representatives on November 14, 2012.

policy that would overextend us and undermine our national security.

To achieve the goals I sought, government would have had to shrink in size and scope, reduce spending, change the monetary system, and reject the unsustainable costs of policing the world and expanding the American Empire.

The problems seemed to be overwhelming and impossible to solve, yet from my viewpoint, just following the constraints placed on the federal government by the Constitution would have been a good place to start.

1. How Much Did I Accomplish?

In many ways, according to conventional wisdom, my off-and-on career in Congress, from 1976 to 2012, accomplished very little. No named legislation, no named federal buildings or highways—thank goodness. In spite of my efforts, the government has grown exponentially, taxes remain excessive, and the prolific increase of incomprehensible regulations continues. Wars are constant and pursued without Congressional declaration, deficits rise to the sky, poverty is rampant and dependency on the federal government is now worse than any time in our history.

All this with minimal concerns for the deficits and unfunded liabilities that common sense tells us cannot go on much longer. A grand, but never mentioned, bipartisan agreement allows for the well-kept secret that keeps the spending going. One side doesn't give up one penny on military spending, the other side doesn't give up one penny on welfare spending, while both sides support the bailouts and subsidies for the banking and corporate elite. And the spending continues as the economy weakens and the downward spiral continues. As the government continues fiddling around, our liberties and our wealth burn in the flames of a foreign policy that makes us less safe.

The major stumbling block to real change in Washington is the total resistance to admitting that the country is broke. This has made compromising, just to agree to increase spending, inevitable since neither side has any intention of cutting spending.

The country and the Congress will remain divisive since there's no "loot left to divvy up."

Without this recognition the spenders in Washington will continue the march toward a fiscal cliff much bigger than the one anticipated this coming January.

I have thought a lot about why those of us who believe in liberty, as a solution, have done so poorly in convincing others of its benefits. If liberty is what we claim it is—the principle that protects all personal, social, and economic decisions necessary for maximum prosperity and the best chance for peace—it should be an easy sell. Yet, history has shown that the masses have been quite receptive to the promises of authoritarians which are rarely if ever fulfilled.

2. Authoritarianism vs. Liberty

If authoritarianism leads to poverty and war and less freedom for all individuals and is controlled by rich special interests, the people should be begging for liberty. There certainly was a strong enough sentiment for more freedom at the time of our founding that motivated those who were willing to fight in the revolution against the powerful British government.

During my time in Congress the appetite for liberty has been quite weak; the understanding of its significance negligible. Yet the good news is that compared to 1976 when I first came to Congress, the desire for more freedom and less government in 2012 is much greater and growing, especially in grassroots America. Tens of thousands of teenagers and college-age students are, with great enthusiasm, welcoming the message of liberty.

I have a few thoughts as to why the people of a country like ours, once the freest and most prosperous, allowed the conditions to deteriorate to the degree that they have.

Freedom, private property, and enforceable voluntary contracts, generate wealth.

In our early history we were very much aware of this. But in the early part of the twentieth century our politicians promoted the notion that the tax and monetary systems had to change if we were to involve ourselves in excessive domestic and military spending. That is why Congress gave us the Federal Reserve and the income tax. The majority of Americans and many government officials agreed that sacrificing some liberty was necessary to carry out what some claimed to be "progressive" ideas. Pure democracy became acceptable.

They failed to recognize that what they were doing was exactly opposite of what the colonists were seeking when they broke away from the British.

Some complain that my arguments makes no sense, since great wealth and the standard of living improved for many Americans over the last 100 years, even with these new policies.

But the damage to the market economy, and the currency, has been insidious and steady. It took a long time to consume our wealth, destroy the currency and undermine productivity, and get our financial obligations to a point of no return. Confidence sometimes lasts longer than deserved. Most of our wealth today depends on debt.

The wealth that we enjoyed and seemed to be endless, allowed concern for the principle of a free society to be neglected. As long as most people believed the material abundance would last forever, worrying about protecting a competitive productive economy and individual liberty seemed unnecessary.

3. The Age of Redistribution

This neglect ushered in an age of redistribution of wealth by government kowtowing to any and all special interests, except for those who just wanted to be left alone. That is why today money in politics far surpasses money currently going into research and development and productive entrepreneurial efforts.

The material benefits became more important than the understanding and promoting the principles of liberty and a free market. It is good that material abundance is a result of liberty but if materialism is all that we care about, problems are guaranteed.

The crisis arrived because the illusion that wealth and prosperity would last forever has ended. Since it was based on debt and a pretense that debt can be papered over by an out-of-control fiat monetary system, it was doomed to fail. We have ended up with a system that doesn't produce enough even to finance the debt and no fundamental understanding of why a free society is crucial to reversing these trends.

If this is not recognized, the recovery will linger for a long time. Bigger government, more spending, more debt, more poverty for the middle class, and a more intense scramble by the elite special interests will continue.

4. We Need an Intellectual Awakening

Without an intellectual awakening, the turning point will be driven by economic law. A dollar crisis will bring the current out-of-control system to its knees.

If it's not accepted that big government, fiat money, ignoring liberty, central economic planning, welfarism, and warfarism caused our crisis we can expect a continuous and dangerous march toward corporatism and even fascism with even more loss of our liberties. Prosperity for a large middle class though will become an abstract dream.

This continuous move is no different than what we have seen in how our financial crisis of 2008 was handled. Congress first directed, with bipartisan support, bailouts for the wealthy. Then it was the Federal Reserve with its endless quantitative easing. If at first it doesn't succeed try again; QE1, QE2, and QE3 and with no results we try QE indefinitely—that is until it too fails. There's a cost to all of this and let me assure you delaying the payment is no longer an option. The rules of the market will extract its pound of flesh and it won't be pretty.

The current crisis elicits a lot of pessimism. And the pessimism adds to less confidence in the future. The two feed on themselves, making our situation worse.

If the underlying cause of the crisis is not understood we cannot solve our problems. The issues of warfare, welfare, deficits, inflationism, corporatism, bailouts and authoritarianism cannot be ignored. By only expanding these policies we cannot expect good results.

Everyone claims support for freedom. But too often it's for one's own freedom and not for others. Too many believe that there must be limits on freedom. They argue that freedom must be directed and managed to achieve fairness and equality thus making it acceptable to curtail, through force, certain liberties.

Some decide what and whose freedoms are to be limited. These are the politicians whose goal in life is power. Their success depends on gaining support from special interests.

5. No More 'isms'

The great news is the answer is not to be found in more "isms." The answers are to be found in more liberty which cost so much less. Under these circumstances spending goes down, wealth production goes up, and the quality of life improves.

Just this recognition—especially if we move in this direction—increases optimism which in itself is beneficial. The follow through with sound policies are required which must be understood and supported by the people.

But there is good evidence that the generation coming of age at the present time is supportive of moving in the direction of more liberty and self-reliance. The more this change in direction and the solutions become known, the quicker will be the return of optimism.

Our job, for those of us who believe that a different system than the one that we have had for the last 100 years, has driven us to this unsustainable crisis, is to be more convincing that there is a wonderful, uncomplicated, and moral system that provides the answers. We had a taste of it in our early history. We need not give up on the notion of advancing this cause.

It worked, but we allowed our leaders to concentrate on the material abundance that freedom generates, while ignoring freedom itself. Now we have neither, but the door is open, out of necessity, for an answer. The answer available is based on the Constitution, individual liberty, and prohibiting the use of government force to provide privileges and benefits to all special interests.

After over 100 years we face a society quite different from the one that was intended by the Founders. In many ways their efforts to protect future generations with the Constitution from this danger has failed. Skeptics, at the time the Constitution was written in 1787, warned us of today's possible outcome. The insidious nature of the erosion of our liberties and the reassurance our great abundance gave us, allowed the process to evolve into the dangerous period in which we now live.

6. Dependency on Government Largesse

Today we face a dependency on government largesse for almost every need. Our liberties are restricted and government operates outside the rule of law, protecting and rewarding those who buy or coerce government into satisfying their demands. Here are a few examples:

- Undeclared wars are commonplace.

- Debt is growing exponentially.

- Welfare for the rich and poor is considered an entitlement.

- Bailouts and guarantees for all kinds of misbehavior are routine.

- Supporters of sanctions, currency manipulation, and WTO trade retaliation, call the true free traders "isolationists."

- Sanctions are used to punish countries that don't follow our orders.

- Tragically our government engages in preemptive war, otherwise known as aggression, with no complaints from the American people.

- Central economic planning through monetary policy, regulations, and legislative mandates has been an acceptable policy.

- The economy is overregulated, overtaxed, and grossly distorted by a deeply flawed monetary system.

- It's now the law of the land that the military can arrest American citizens, hold them indefinitely, without charges or a trial.

- Rampant hostility toward free trade is supported by a large number in Washington.

- The drone warfare we are pursuing worldwide is destined to end badly for the U.S. as the hatred builds for innocent lives lost and the international laws flaunted. Once we are financially weakened and militarily challenged, there will be a lot of resentment thrown our way.

- The Patriot Act and FISA legislation passed without much debate have resulted in a steady erosion of our 4th Amendment rights.

7. Questions

Excessive government has created such a mess it prompts many questions:

- Why are sick people who use medical marijuana put in prison?

- Why does the federal government restrict the drinking of raw milk?

- Why can't Americans manufacture rope and other products from hemp?

- Why are Americans not allowed to use gold and silver as legal tender as mandated by the Constitution?

- Why do our political leaders believe it's unnecessary to thoroughly audit our own gold?

- Why can't Americans decide which type of light bulbs they can buy?

- Why is the TSA permitted to abuse the rights of any American traveling by air?

- Why should there be mandatory sentences—even up to life for crimes without victims—as our drug laws require?

- Why is Germany concerned enough to consider repatriating their gold held by the FED for her in New York? Is it that the trust in the U.S. and dollar supremacy is beginning to wane?

- Why have we allowed the federal government to regulate commodes in our homes?

- Why is it political suicide for anyone to criticize AIPAC ?

- Why haven't we given up on the drug war since it's an obvious failure and violates the people's rights? Has nobody noticed that the authorities can't even keep drugs out of the prisons? How can making our entire society a prison solve the problem?

- Why do we sacrifice so much getting needlessly involved in border disputes and civil strife around the world and ignore the root cause of the most deadly border in the world—the one between Mexico and the U.S.?

- Why does changing the party in power never change policy? Could it be that the views of both parties are essentially the same?

- Why did the big banks, the large corporations, and foreign banks and foreign central banks get bailed out in 2008 and the middle class lost their jobs and their homes?

- Why do so many accept the deeply flawed principle that government bureaucrats and politicians can protect us from ourselves without totally destroying the principle of liberty?

- Why do so many in the government and the federal officials believe that creating money out of thin air creates wealth?

- Why does Congress willingly give up its prerogatives to the Executive Branch?

- Why can't people understand that war always destroys wealth and liberty?

- Why did we ever give the government a safe haven for initiating violence against the people?

- Why is patriotism thought to be blind loyalty to the government and the politicians who run it, rather than loyalty to the principles of liberty and support for the people? Real patriotism is a willingness to challenge the government when it's wrong.

- Why do some members defend free markets, but not civil liberties?

- Why do some members defend civil liberties but not free markets? Aren't they the same?

- Why is there so little concern for the Executive Order that gives the President authority to establish a "kill list," including American citizens, of those targeted for assassination?

- Why don't more defend both economic liberty and personal liberty?

- Why is it claimed that if people won't or can't take care of their own needs, that people in government can do it for them?

- Why are there not more individuals who seek to intellectually influence others to bring about positive changes than those who seek power to force others to obey their commands?

- Why do we allow the government and the Federal Reserve to disseminate false information dealing with both economic and foreign policy?

- Why is democracy held in such high esteem when it's the enemy of the minority and makes all rights relative to the dictates of the majority?

- Why should anyone be surprised that Congress has no credibility, since there's such a disconnect between

what politicians say and what they
do?

- Why does the use of religion to support a social gospel and preemptive
  wars, both of which requires authoritarians to use violence, or the
  threat of violence, go unchallenged?
  Aggression and forced redistribution
  of wealth has nothing to do with
  the teachings of the world great religions.

- Is there any explanation for all the
  deception, the unhappiness, the fear
  of the future, the loss of confidence
  in our leaders, the distrust, the anger and frustration? Yes there is, and
  there's a way to reverse these attitudes. The negative perceptions are
  logical and a consequence of bad
  policies bringing about our problems. Identification of the problems
  and recognizing the cause allow the
  proper changes to come easy.

8. Trust Yourself, Not the Government

Too many people have for too long placed too much confidence and trust in government and not enough in themselves. Fortunately, many are now becoming aware of the seriousness of the gross mistakes of the past several decades. The blame is shared by both political parties. Many Americans now are demanding to hear the plain truth of things and want the demagoguing to stop. Without this first step, solutions are impossible.

Seeking the truth and finding the answers in liberty and self-reliance promotes the optimism necessary for restoring prosperity. The task is not that difficult if politics doesn't get in the way.

We have allowed ourselves to get into such a mess for various reasons.

Politicians deceive themselves as to how wealth is produced. Excessive confidence is placed in the judgment of politicians and bureaucrats. This replaces the confidence in a free society. Too many in high places of authority became convinced that only they, armed with arbitrary government power, can bring about fairness, while facilitating wealth production. This always proves to be a utopian dream and destroys wealth and liberty. It impoverishes the people and rewards the special interests who end up controlling both political parties.

It's no surprise then that much of what goes on in Washington is driven by aggressive partisanship and power seeking, with philosophic differences being minor.

9. Economic Ignorance

Economic ignorance is commonplace. Keynesianism continues to thrive, although today it is facing healthy and enthusiastic rebuttals. Believers in military Keynesianism and domestic Keynesianism continue to desperately promote their failed policies, as the economy languishes in a deep slumber.

Supporters of all government edicts use humanitarian arguments to justify them.

Humanitarian arguments are always used to justify government mandates related to the economy, monetary policy, foreign policy, and personal liberty. This is on purpose to make it more difficult to challenge. But, initiating violence for humanitarian reasons is still violence. Good intentions are no excuse and are just as harmful as when people use force with bad intentions. The results are always negative.

The immoral use of force is the source of man's political problems. Sadly, many religious groups, secular organizations, and psychopathic authoritarians endorse government initiated force to change the world. Even when the desired goals are well-intentioned—or especially when well-intentioned—the results are dismal. The good results sought never materialize. The new problems created require even more government force as a solution. The net result is institutionalizing government initiated violence and morally justifying it on humanitarian grounds.

This is the same fundamental reason our government uses force for invading other countries at will, central economic planning at home, and the regulation of personal liberty and habits of our citizens.

It is rather strange, that unless one has a criminal mind and no respect for other people and their property, no one claims it's permissible to go into one's neighbor's house and tell them how to behave, what they can eat, smoke and drink or how to spend their money.

Yet, rarely is it asked why it is morally acceptable that a stranger with a badge and a gun can do the same thing in the name of law and order. Any resistance is met with brute force, fines, taxes, arrests, and even imprisonment. This is done more frequently every day without a proper search warrant.

10. No Government Monopoly over Initiating Violence

Restraining aggressive behavior is one thing, but legalizing a government monopoly for initiating aggression can only lead to exhausting liberty associated with chaos, anger, and the breakdown of civil society.

Permitting such authority and expecting saintly behavior from the bureaucrats and the politicians is a pipe dream. We now have a standing army of armed bureaucrats in the TSA, CIA, FBI, Fish and Wildlife, FEMA, IRS, Corp of Engineers, etc., numbering over 100,000. Citizens are guilty until proven innocent in the unconstitutional administrative courts.

Government in a free society should have no authority to meddle in social activities or the economic transactions of individuals. Nor should government meddle in the affairs of other nations. All things peaceful, even when controversial, should be permitted.

We must reject the notion of prior restraint in economic activity just as we do in the area of free speech and religious liberty. But even in these areas government is starting to use a backdoor approach of political correctness to regulate speech—a dangerous trend. Since 9/11 monitoring speech on the internet is now a problem since warrants are no longer required.

11. The Proliferation of Federal Crimes

The Constitution established four federal crimes. Today the experts can't even agree on how many federal crimes are now on the books—they number into the thousands. No one person can comprehend the enormity of the legal system—especially the tax code. Due to the ill-advised drug war and the endless federal expansion of the criminal code we have over 6 million people under correctional suspension, more than the Soviets ever had, and more than any other nation today, including China. I don't understand the complacency of the Congress and the willingness to continue their obsession with passing more Federal laws. Mandatory sentencing laws associated with drug laws have compounded our prison problems.

The federal register is now 75,000 pages long and the tax code has 72,000 pages, and expands every year. When will the people start shouting, "enough is enough," and demand Congress cease and desist.

12. Achieving Liberty

Liberty can only be achieved when government is denied the aggressive use of force. If one seeks liberty, a precise type of government is needed. To achieve it, more than lip service is required.

Two choices are available.

1. A government designed to protect liberty—a natural right—as its sole objective. The people are expected to care for themselves and reject the use of any force for interfering with another person's liberty. Government is given a strictly limited authority to enforce contracts, property ownership, settle disputes, and defend against foreign aggression.

2. A government that pretends to protect liberty but is granted power to arbitrarily use force over the people and foreign nations. Though the grant of power many times is meant to be small and limited, it inevitably metastasizes into an omnipotent

political cancer. This is the problem for which the world has suffered throughout the ages. Though meant to be limited it nevertheless is a 100 percent sacrifice of a principle that would-be-tyrants find irresistible. It is used vigorously—though incrementally and insidiously. Granting power to government officials always proves the adage that: "power corrupts."

Once government gets a limited concession for the use of force to mold people's habits and plan the economy, it causes a steady move toward tyrannical government. Only a revolutionary spirit can reverse the process and deny to the government this arbitrary use of aggression. There's no in-between. Sacrificing a little liberty for imaginary safety always ends badly.

Today's mess is a result of Americans accepting option #2, even though the Founders attempted to give us Option #1.

The results are not good. As our liberties have been eroded our wealth has been consumed. The wealth we see today is based on debt and a foolish willingness on the part of foreigners to take our dollars for goods and services. They then loan them back to us to perpetuate our debt system. It's amazing that it has worked for this long but the impasse in Washington, in solving our problems indicate that many are starting to understand the seriousness of the world-wide debt crisis and the dangers we face. The longer this process continues the harsher the outcome will be.

13. The Financial Crisis Is a Moral Crisis

Many are now acknowledging that a financial crisis looms but few understand it's, in reality, a moral crisis. It's the moral crisis that has allowed our liberties to be undermined and permits the exponential growth of illegal government power. Without a clear understanding of the nature of the crisis it will be difficult to prevent a steady march toward tyranny and the poverty that will accompany it.

Ultimately, the people have to decide which form of government they want; option #1 or option #2. There is no other choice. Claiming there is a choice of a "little" tyranny is like describing pregnancy as a "touch of pregnancy." It is a myth to believe that a mixture of free markets and government central economic planning is a worthy compromise. What we see today is a result of that type of thinking. And the results speak for themselves.

14. A Culture of Violence

America now suffers from a culture of violence. It's easy to reject the initiation of violence against one's neighbor but it's ironic that the people arbitrarily and freely anoint government officials with monopoly power to initiate violence against the American people—practically at will.

Because it's the government that initiates force, most people accept it as being legitimate. Those who exert the force have no sense of guilt. It is believed by too many that governments are morally justified in initiating force supposedly to "do good." They incorrectly believe that this authority has come from the "consent of the people." The minority, or victims of government violence never consented to suffer the abuse of government mandates, even when dictated by the majority. Victims of TSA excesses never consented to this abuse.

This attitude has given us a policy of initiating war to "do good," as well. It is claimed that war, to prevent war for noble purposes, is justified. This is similar to what we were once told that: "destroying a village to save a village" was justified. It was said by a U.S. Secretary of State that the loss of 500,000 Iraqis, mostly children, in the 1990s, as a result of American bombs and sanctions, was "worth it" to achieve the "good" we brought to the Iraqi people. And look at the mess that Iraq is in today.

Government use of force to mold social and economic behavior at home and

abroad has justified individuals using force
on their own terms. The fact that violence
by government is seen as morally justified, is
the reason why violence will increase when
the big financial crisis hits and becomes a
political crisis as well.

First, we recognize that individuals
shouldn't initiate violence, then we give
the authority to government. Eventually,
the immoral use of government violence,
when things go badly, will be used to justify
an individual's "right" to do the same thing.
Neither the government nor individuals
have the moral right to initiate violence
against another yet we are moving toward
the day when both will claim this authority. If this cycle is not reversed society will
break down.

When needs are pressing, conditions deteriorate and rights become relative to the
demands and the whims of the majority. It's
then not a great leap for individuals to take
it upon themselves to use violence to get
what they claim is theirs. As the economy
deteriorates and the wealth discrepancies

increase—as are already occurring—violence increases as those in need take it in their own hands to get what they believe is theirs. They will not wait for a government rescue program.

When government officials wield power over others to bail out the special interests, even with disastrous results to the average citizen, they feel no guilt for the harm they do. Those who take us into undeclared wars with many casualties resulting, never lose sleep over the death and destruction their bad decisions caused. They are convinced that what they do is morally justified, and the fact that many suffer just can't be helped.

When the street criminals do the same thing, they too have no remorse, believing they are only taking what is rightfully theirs. All moral standards become relative. Whether it's bailouts, privileges, government subsidies or benefits for some from inflating a currency, it's all part of a process justified by a philosophy of forced redistribution of wealth. Violence, or a threat of such, is the instrument required and unfortunately is of little concern of most members of Congress.

Some argue it's only a matter of "fairness" that those in need are cared for. There are two problems with this. First, the principle is used to provide a greater amount of benefits to the rich than to the poor. Second, no one seems to be concerned about whether or not it's fair to those who end up paying for the benefits. The costs are usually placed on the backs of the middle class and are hidden from the public eye. Too many people believe government handouts are free, like printing money out of thin air, and there is no cost. That deception is coming to an end. The bills are coming due and that's what the economic slowdown is all about.

Sadly, we have become accustomed to living with the illegitimate use of force by government. It is the tool for telling the people how to live, what to eat and drink, what to read and how to spend their money.

To develop a truly free society, the issue of initiating force must be understood and rejected. Granting to government even a small amount of force is a dangerous concession.

15. Limiting Government Excesses vs. A Virtuous Moral People

Our Constitution, which was intended to limit government power and abuse, has failed. The Founders warned that a free society depends on a virtuous and moral people. The current crisis reflects that their concerns were justified.

Most politicians and pundits are aware of the problems we face but spend all their time in trying to reform government. The sad part is that the suggested reforms almost always lead to less freedom and the importance of a virtuous and moral people is either ignored, or not understood. The new reforms serve only to further undermine liberty. The compounding effect has given us this steady erosion of liberty and the massive expansion of debt. The real question is: if it is liberty we seek, should most of the emphasis be placed on government reform or trying to understand what "a virtuous and moral people" means and how to promote it? The Constitution has not prevented the people from demanding handouts for both rich and poor in their efforts to reform the government, while ignoring the principles of a free society. All branches of our government today are controlled by individuals who use their power to undermine liberty and enhance the welfare/warfare state—and frequently their own wealth and power.

If the people are unhappy with the government performance it must be recognized that government is merely a reflection of an immoral society that rejected a moral government of constitutional limitations of power and love of freedom.

If this is the problem all the tinkering with thousands of pages of new laws and regulations will do nothing to solve the problem.

It is self-evident that our freedoms have been severely limited and the apparent prosperity we still have, is nothing more than leftover wealth from a previous time. This fictitious wealth based on debt and benefits from a false trust in our currency and credit, will play havoc with our society when the bills come due. This means that the full consequence of our lost liberties is yet to be felt.

But that illusion is now ending. Reversing a downward spiral depends on accepting a new approach.

Expect the rapidly expanding home-schooling movement to play a significant role in the revolutionary reforms needed to build a free society with Constitutional protections. We cannot expect a Federal government controlled school system to provide the intellectual ammunition to combat the dangerous growth of government that threatens our liberties.

The internet will provide the alternative to the government/media complex that controls the news and most political propaganda. This is why it's essential that the internet remains free of government regulation.

Many of our religious institutions and secular organizations support greater dependency on the state by supporting war, welfare, and corporatism and ignore the need for a virtuous people.

I never believed that the world or our country could be made more free by politicians, if the people had no desire for freedom.

Under the current circumstances the most we can hope to achieve in the political process is to use it as a podium to reach the people to alert them of the nature of the crisis and the importance of their need to assume responsibility for themselves, if it is liberty that they truly seek. Without this, a constitutionally protected free society is impossible.

If this is true, our individual goal in life ought to be for us to seek virtue and excellence and recognize that self-esteem and happiness only comes from using one's natural ability, in the most productive manner possible, according to one's own talents.

Productivity and creativity are the true source of personal satisfaction. Freedom, and not dependency, provides the environment needed to achieve these goals. Government cannot do this for us; it only gets in the way. When the government gets involved, the goal becomes a bailout or a subsidy and these cannot provide a sense of personal achievement.

Achieving legislative power and political influence should not be our goal. Most of the change, if it is to come, will not come from the politicians, but rather from individuals, family, friends, intellectual leaders and our religious institutions. The solution can only come from rejecting the use of coercion, compulsion, government commands, and aggressive force, to mold social and economic behavior. Without accepting these restraints, inevitably the consensus will be to allow the government to mandate economic equality and obedience to the politicians who gain power and promote an environment that smothers the freedoms of everyone. It is then that the responsible individuals who seek excellence and self-esteem by being self-reliant and productive, become the true victims.

16. Conclusion

What are the greatest dangers that the American people face today and impede the goal of a free society? There are five.

1. The continuous attack on our civil liberties which threatens the rule of law and our ability to resist the on-rush of tyranny.

2. Violent anti-Americanism that has engulfed the world. Because the phenomenon of "blow-back" is not understood or denied, our foreign policy is destined to keep us involved in many wars that we have no business being in. National bankruptcy and a greater threat to our national security will result.

3. The ease in which we go to war, without a declaration by Congress, but accepting international authority from the UN or NATO even for preemptive wars, otherwise known as aggression.

4. A financial political crisis as a consequence of excessive debt, unfunded liabilities, spending, bailouts, and gross discrepancy in wealth distribution going from the middle class to the rich. The danger of central economic planning, by the Federal Reserve must be understood.

5. World government taking over local and U.S. sovereignty by getting involved in the issues of war, welfare, trade, banking, a world currency, taxes, property ownership, and private ownership of guns. Happily, there is an answer for these very dangerous trends.

What a wonderful world it would be if everyone accepted the simple moral premise of rejecting all acts of aggression. The retort to such a suggestion is always: it's too simplistic, too idealistic, impractical, naïve, utopian, dangerous, and unrealistic to strive for such an ideal.

The answer to that is that for thousands of years the acceptance of government force, to rule over the people, at the sacrifice of liberty, was considered moral and the only available option for achieving peace and prosperity.

What could be more utopian than that myth—considering the results especially looking at the state sponsored killing, by nearly every government during the twentieth century, estimated to be in the hundreds of millions. It's time to reconsider this grant of authority to the state.

No good has ever come from granting monopoly power to the state to use aggression against the people to arbitrarily mold human behavior. Such power, when left unchecked, becomes the seed of an ugly tyranny. This method of governance has been adequately tested, and the results are in: reality dictates we try liberty.

The idealism of non-aggression and rejecting all offensive use of force should be tried. The idealism of government sanctioned violence has been abused throughout history and is the primary source of poverty and war. The theory of a society being based on individual freedom has been around for a long time. It's time to take a bold step and actually permit it by advancing this cause, rather than taking a step backward as some would like us to do.

Today the principle of *habeas corpus*, established when King John signed the Magna Carta in 1215, is under attack. There's every reason to believe that a renewed effort with the use of the internet can instead advance the cause of liberty by spreading an uncensored message that will serve to rein in government authority and challenge the obsession with war and welfare.

What I'm talking about is a system of government guided by the moral principles of peace and tolerance.

The Founders were convinced that a free society could not exist without a moral people. Just writing rules won't work if the people choose to ignore them. Today the rule of law written in the Constitution has little meaning for most Americans, especially those who work in Washington, D.C.

Benjamin Franklin claimed "only a virtuous people are capable of freedom." John Adams concurred: "Our Constitution was made for a moral and religious people. It is wholly inadequate to the government of any other."

A moral people must reject all violence in an effort to mold people's beliefs or habits.

A society that boos or ridicules the Golden Rule is not a moral society. All great religions endorse the Golden Rule. The same moral standards that individuals are required to follow should apply to all government officials. They cannot be exempt.

The ultimate solution is not in the hands of the government.

The solution falls on each and every individual, with guidance from family, friends, and community.

The #1 responsibility for each of us is to change ourselves with hope that others will follow. This is of greater importance than working on changing the government; that is secondary to promoting a virtuous society. If we can achieve this, then the government will change.

It doesn't mean that political action or holding office has no value. At times it does nudge policy in the right direction. But what is true is that when seeking office is done for personal aggrandizement, money or power, it becomes useless if not harmful. When political action is taken for the right reasons it's easy to understand why compromise should be avoided. It also becomes clear why progress is best achieved by working with coalitions, which bring people together, without anyone sacrificing his principles.

Political action, to be truly beneficial, must be directed toward changing the hearts and minds of the people, recognizing that it's the virtue and morality of the people that allow liberty to flourish.

The Constitution or more laws per se, have no value if the people's attitudes aren't changed.

To achieve liberty and peace, two powerful human emotions have to be overcome. Number one is "envy" which leads to hate and class warfare. Number two is "intolerance" which leads to bigoted and judgmental policies. These emotions must be replaced with a much better understanding of love, compassion, tolerance, and free market economics. Freedom, when understood, brings people together. When tried, freedom is popular.

The problem we have faced over the years has been that economic interventionists are swayed by envy, whereas social interventionists are swayed by intolerance of habits and lifestyles. The misunderstanding that tolerance is an endorsement of certain activities, motivates many to legislate moral standards which should only be set by individuals making their own choices. Both sides use force to deal with these misplaced emotions. Both are authoritarians. Neither endorses voluntarism. Both views ought to be rejected.

I have come to one firm conviction after these many years of trying to figure out "the plain truth of things." The best chance for achieving peace and prosperity, for the maximum number of people world-wide, is to pursue the cause of LIBERTY.

If you find this to be a worthwhile message, spread it throughout the land.